LEADING A LOCAL UNITED METHODIST CHURCH

A LEADERSHIP MANUAL FOR THE USE OF LOCAL CHURCHES IN THE LIBERIA ANNUAL CONFERENCE OF THE UNITED METHODIST CHURCH

REV. DR. JULIUS Y.Z.K. WILLIAMS, I

First Published in 2017

Published by:
FORTE Publications
#12 Ashmun Street
Snapper Hill
Monrovia, Liberia
[+231-881-106-177]

FORTE Publishing
7202 Tavenner Lane
208 Alexandria
VA, 22306
+1-571-332-5782]

FORTE Press
76 Sarasit Road
Ban Pong, 70110
Ratchaburi, Thailand
+66-85-824-4382

http://fortepublishing.wix.com/fppp
fortepublishing@gmail.com

Printed in the United States of America

ISBN-13: 978-0994630834
ISBN-10: 0994630832

Rev. Dr. Julius Y.Z.K. Williams, I
A Clergy member of the Liberia Annual Conference of the United Methodist Church

Leading a Local United Methodist Church
A Leadership Manual for the Use of Local Churches in the LAC/UMC

DEDICATION

To The Liberia Annual Conference,
The United Methodist Church (LAC/UMC);

To the Leaders and Members of the
First United Methodist Church (FUMC-Monrovia).

FOREWORD

Rev. Dr. Julius Y. Z. K. Williams, I has spent a good portion of his life and energy in pastoring congregations of The United Methodist Church in the Liberia Annual Conference. Through his doctoral research work and many leadership seminars he has held with local churches around our conference, he has discovered a dire need for a leadership manual to be placed within reach of every local church leader in our conference. The scarcity of this particular leadership tool is having a negative impact on the temporal life of many of our local churches.

This small leadership manual is his own way of helping to alleviate this acute problem. In it, Dr. Williams has set out to accomplish only one thing; that of aiding the local church leadership—both minister and lay—"to know how the local United Methodist church works". It lays out a basic understanding of the local church, its ministries, their functions, with special emphasis on the church council, its make-up, and what is expected of its members.

Though small, I advise readers not to read it in one sitting like a novel. Each chapter deals with a different topic and so should be read according to the person's need. One thing is obvious; and that is its easy-to-understand language and straight-to-the-point discussion on common problems. There are even discussion questions at the end of every chapter.

I recommend that every local church leader—both clergy and lay—get a copy and treat it like a basic student manual for church leadership in the United Methodist Church.

Rev. Dr. Yatta Roslyn Young
Dean
United Methodist University
Graduate School of Theology

CONTENTS

HE LEADETH ME: O BLESSED THOUGHT

He leadeth me: O blessed thought! O words with heavenly comfort fraught whate'er I do, where'er I be, Still 'tis God's hand that leadeth me.

REFRAIN: He leadeth, he leadeth me, by his own hand he leadeth me; His faithful follower I would be, For by his hand he leadeth me.

Sometimes mid scenes of deepest gloom, sometimes where Eden's bowers bloom, by waters still, o'er troubled sea, still
'tis his hand that leadeth me. REFRAIN

Lord, I would place my hand in thine, nor ever murmur nor repine; content, whatever lot I see, since 'tis my God that leadeth me. REFRAIN

And when my task on earth is done, when by thy grace the victory's won, e'en death's cold wave I will not flee, since God through Jordan leadeth me. REFRAIN

**The hymn was written by Joseph H. Gilmore and music by William B. Bradbury.

As you take your journey through this manual, kindly prayerfully sing the below hymn:

TAKE MY LIFE, AND LET IT BE CONSECRATED

Take my life, and let it be consecrated, Lord to, to thee. Take my moments and my days; let them flow in cease-less praise. Take my hands, and let them move at the impulse of thy love. Take my feet, and let them be swift and beautiful for thee.

Take my voice, and let me sing always, only, for my King. Take my lips, and let them be filled with messages from thee. Take my silver and my gold; not a mite would I withhold. Take my intellect, and use every power as thou shalt choose.

Take my will, and make it thine; it shall be no longer mine. Take my heart, it is thine own; it shall be thy royal throne. Take my love, my Lord; I pour at thy feet its treasure store. Take myself, and I will be ever, only all for thee.

INTRODUCTION

(WHAT IS THIS UNITED METHODIST LEADERSHIP MANUAL ALL ABOUT?)

Even though The United Methodist Church is a part of the Christian community worldwide, it is a unique denomination in the world.

My doctoral research work and leadership seminars conducted in three districts of the Liberia Annual Conference of The United Methodist Church revealed that most of our leaders and members need to have adequate knowledge of the local church, its ministries and their functions as well as the responsibilities of the church council.

United Methodists have the desire to better understand and serve their churches. The big challenge, especially for pastors, is the availability of the necessary leadership tool to equip and empower them and the laity.

The Book of Discipline of The United Methodist Church, which is the book that governs our church, is in short supply in LAC/UMC. Only few clergy and lay persons are opportune to have this book. Less than one percent of United Methodists has access to the law book of the United Methodist Church.

If local churches must do well in carrying out meaningful ministries in their communities and beyond, there must be an alternative to fill the gap created as a result of the scarcity of the Book of Discipline and other leadership tools. And that alternative is to prepare a leadership manual. It is this lack of leadership resource materials that has led me to do this manual for both the clergy and the laity.

It is my prayer and hope that this resource material will help our people effectively and efficiently carry out their responsibilities given them by the bishop and the pastors.

This material may not be in depth, but I am sure it will give you some understanding of how the local United Methodist Church operates.

United Methodists are people of methods. Therefore, those who lead the church should follow the guidelines that have been documented by fellow United Methodists.

As United Methodists, we must desire to deepen our knowledge of the workings of our dear church. We must all strive to know where we are. Knowing the functions of the local church and its leadership will give us a better understanding of how to do ministries. United Methodist polity is different from that of other denominations. The United Methodist Church cannot and will not operate a charismatic form of government.

This manual is designed to help those who want to know how the local United Methodist Church works. It is divided into six chapters.

Chapter One focuses on leadership. Secular leadership and biblical leadership are discussed in this chapter. A brief comparative analysis of the kinds of leadership is also looked at. Further, the section closes with who a leader is and the qualities of a Christian leader.

Chapter Two looks at the local church, its functions, and authority. The focus here is to look at different definitions of a church, the work the church has to do and to examine the power of God's church here on earth.

Chapter Three discusses pastoral leadership in a local church. It opens our minds to who a pastor is and the responsibilities he or she has. Also the restrictions that each pastor has in carrying out ministry activity are discussed.

Chapter Four looks at the diversities of congregations. It takes into consideration the essence of congregating, congregations in the Old and New Testaments, different congregations as well as seeing the pastor as the pacesetter of the congregation.

Chapter Five focuses on who becomes a member of the leadership team in a local church.

Chapter Six takes a look at the church council and its responsibilities. In this, ministry and mission, the meeting, the membership, and the quorum of the council are discussed.

Chapter Seven looks at the lay leader and the chairperson of the council. These are two key servant leaders that are worth discussing. Their functions are outlined in this section.

Chapter Eight talks about the administrative and support committees and ministries of the local United Methodist Church. Detailed information is outlined in this chapter.

Chapter Nine discusses the five important groupings in any local United Methodist church: men, women, young adults, youth and children ministry.

Let me express my gratitude to you readers for taking time off to learn a little about a local United Methodist Church. Enjoy your learning journey of the local UMC.

A renowned United Methodist, Charles Wesley in the eighteen century wrote:

A charge to keep I have, a God to glorify,
a never dying soul to save, and fit it for the sky.

To serve the present age, my calling to fulfill;
O may it all my power engage to do my master's will!

Arm me with jealous care, as in thy sight to live, and oh, thy servant, Lord, prepare a strict account to give!

Help me to watch and pray, and on thyself rely, assured, if I my trust betray, I shall forever die.

We are United Methodists and we will remain United Methodists. May the blessings of the Lord rest upon you as you read.

Leadership

CHAPTER 1

LEADERSHIP

Leadership is critical to the survival and growth of any institution, especially in the church, based on the following:

> It is the life blood for ministry (ies) in any local church. The local church moves in the direction of its leaders. For instance, ducklings follow Mother Duck; wherever she goes, the ducklings follow. Thus, when the local church leadership has a problem, the church is also troubled.

When the leadership lacks vision, the local church experiences no spiritual or temporal growth. The kind of leadership that is practiced at a local church determines where the church is headed.

> Leadership has the ability to build or break any institution. Leadership has the grace to ensure that an institution moves from stage one to stage two. In the simplest form, growth, development and the up-liftment of the church has to with leadership. On the other hand, for the organization not to move forward to the place where God intends to move the institution is dependent upon leadership. The leadership can just decide to say things will not work; and of course it will not work because it is the leadership that ensures that the institution move forward.

However, the church is not just any organization. Leaders are required by faith and belief to care for and/or love everyone. This singular dimension sets it apart from secular leadership where the standards don't have to cross the professional or normal human tenets of the civilized world. It renders church leadership not just academic or professional but faith based. It is a key ingredient of religion. And this, church leaders understand fully well. They are ever conscious of the underlying conditions of their leadership roles and decisions. They are aware that they must extend any decision or action well beyond the professional and academic level.

What is Leadership?

Leadership is hard to define in a way that is universally acceptable. Leadership can be defined from different perspectives. As we look at some definitions, we will consider the meaning of leadership from the following angles as:

service,
guidance,
an *office*,
vocation,
directional and
people-oriented.

Leadership is Service.

Service is often not considered with the level of importance it should have when treating the issue with leadership. However, Christ showed us the importance of service to a good leader. He exemplified this on several occasions most notably when he washed the feet of his disciples or stopped to acknowledge the woman that had touched Him in the midst of the crowd and received her healing. In His many parables, the issue of service played a major role.

As leaders, we are servants first. We serve those we lead. It is only through our service that we become good leaders. By service, we master the skills we need to lead. We master things like patience, care, understanding and humility.

By service, we also improve our communication

Leadership is Guidance.

It is the ability to take people from their known world to the unknown; and the capacity to lead people or an institution to meet the desired results. When leading people, one must gain their trust. It is easier to move from known to unknown because we are more comfortable with the familiar. We based our learning on the known and then grow it. Thus, a good leader endeavors to lead or guide the process.

Leadership is an Office

Someone once said that leadership is simply the office of the leader. Leadership being an office carries certain implications. Implicit therein is the notion that leaders owe a duty of service to those being led. As an office, one is constantly reminded of the task at hand.

Leadership is a Vocation

Leadership is "a vocation which blends both human and divine qualities in a harmony of ministry by God and his people for the blessings of others.[1]

One the one hand there is the general belief that all leadership comes from God and then there is the belief that leadership is a calling.

As a vocation, God personally calls one into leadership. This places primacy on the calling as a duty to God first than others afterwards. This logic furthers that, since God calls leaders to lead, they must lead along to the tenets He has set.

Leadership is Directional

It is also defined as "the development and articulation of a shared vision, motivation of those key people without whom that vision cannot become a reality and gaining the cooperation of most of the people involved".[2]

Leadership is People Oriented

Leadership involves dealing with people. No people, no leadership. This means that no one leads when there is no one to follow. It is about followership.

Biblical Leadership

Leadership is seen from two perspectives: secular as well as

---

[1] J. Oswald Sanders, *Spiritual Leadership: Principles of Excellence for Every Believer* (Illinois: Oasis International Ltd., 1967), 28.

[2] Lovett H. Weems, Jr., *Church Leadership: Vision, Team, Culture Integrity* (Nashville: Abingdon Press, 1993), 12.

biblical. Biblical leadership talks about a leadership that is under the control and influence of the Holy Spirit. God seeks young people, men and women who will serve him with their whole heart. Simply put, this is leadership based solely on biblical principles.

What is Biblical Leadership?

Leadership based on biblical principles can be looked at from different areas. In this section, the key consideration is biblical leadership as a sincere Christian service, spiritual, corrective, connective, convincing, and emotional.

> Jesus said, *"Whoever wants to be great among you will be your servant. Whoever wants to be first among you will be your slave – just as the Human One didn't come to be served but rather to serve and to give his life to liberate many people"*(Matthew 20: 26-28).

Sincere

> Biblical leadership is sincere Christian service. As mentioned above, it is service oriented. An underlying driver of biblical leader[ship] is its/his/her ability to turn every opportunity into or toward service.

Spiritual

- A leadership that is spiritual in nature and centered in God; as believers, we know that God is the essence of our existence. As we struggle with the existential questions in life, we take comfort in knowing that our souls are God's and our spirits are His to lead.

Corrective

A leadership aimed at meaningful change. The change here transcends the normal. It focuses on the correctiveness of the situation. By so doing, God leads this change process, which then refines and produces a better result than that which existed.

Connective

A leadership that moves people on to God's agenda.[3] We all understand the importance of networking in our modern society. When we connect we expand our network. We grow, and the chances of us getting better are far higher. If ours is a business that depends on numbers, when we network well, we most likely increase that number into something meaningful. Same is true for God. By connecting with Him, we don't only grow spiritually, we grow in all other aspects of our lives. God then becomes the rock or platform from which we grow. He becomes the source form which we nurture others.

Convincing

A leadership that convinces others not by the power of the leader's personality, but that personality initiated, interpenetrated, and empowered by the Holy Spirit.[4]

---

[3] Henry & Richard Blackaby, *Spiritual Leadership* (Nashville: B & H Publishing Group, 2001), 20.
[4] Sanders, *Spiritual Leadership: Principles of Excellence for Every Believer*, 28.

Emotional

It is not an affair of the head; it is an affair of the heart. Our emotions have proven to not always be the best place to make decisions.

Some differences between secular leadership and biblical leadership[5]

Secular Leadership	Biblical Leadership
The leader places confidence in him/herself	The leader places confidence in God
The leader is known by people and he or she knows people	The leader knows God as well as people
The leader does not depend on God to make decisions	The leader depends on God to make decisions. God's will is best for her/him
The leader is independent	The leader is God-dependent
The leader relies on his or her education	The leader relies on the wisdom of God
The leader is personality-driven	The leader is god-driven
The leader is not led by the Holy Spirit	The leader is led by the Holy Spirit.
The leader seeks to give glory to people	The leader seeks to give glory to God
The leader seeks worldly applause	The leader seeks God's approval

[5] Ibid, 29.

Who is a leader?

Individuals look at a leader from different viewpoints. Some see a leader as the chief; and without him or her, the group cannot move forward. A leader whether in the sacred or secular community plays a pivotal role.

Let us look at a few definitions by famous people of who a leader is:

From Famous People

- John R. Mott: "a leader is a man (or woman) who knows the road, who can keep ahead, and who pulls others after him or her."[6]

- President Harry S. Truman: "A leader is a person who has the ability to get others to do what they don't want to do and like it".[7]
- A person who has the ability to take others to the next level.

Anonymous People:

- "Someone or something that leads or is able to lead."
- "a person who leads such as a guide or conductor."

Personal definitions

- A person who has the ability to take others to the next level.

- A leader is a visionary.

- His or her dreams take the group to where it ought to be.

---

[6] J. Oswald Sanders, *Spiritual Leadership: Commitment to Spiritual Growth Series*(Chicago: The Moody Press, 1993), 28.
[7] Ibid, 28.

a. A leader is a visionary.

- His or her dreaming takes the group to where it ought to be.

b. Who is a biblical leader?

A biblical leader is not a secular leader. She/he does not lead as the people in the world lead. Let us consider few insights:

- A person who has received Jesus the Christ as his or her personal Lord and Savior.

- A person whose life is crucified with Jesus the Christ (Phil.1:21).

- A person who allows Christ to lead him or her in leading
- God's people.

- A person who is a mature convert, a disciple, a mentor who is in charge of God's people.

- A person who allows the Holy Spirit, the Third Person of the Trinity, to guide him/her in leading.

- A person who knows that he or she is accountable to God.

- "Someone who is called by God to lead; leads with and through Christlike character; and demonstrates the functional competencies that permit effective leadership to take place."[8]

---

[8] George Barna, *Leaders of Leadership* (California: Regal Books, 1997), 25.

c. Some qualities of a Christian leader

A Christian leader is not just anyone. He or she should possess certain qualities. Below are few qualities that are found in a true Christian leader:

- Christ is at the center of the leader's life(Gal.2:20; Phi.1:21)
- Morally upright.
- A student of the Word of God (Ezra 7:10, II Timothy 2:15).
- A person of prayers (I Thessalonians 5:17).
- Love for God and others(John 13:34-35)
- A leader should be unselfish and generous, willing to open his or her dwelling place for ministry and to share his/her earthly blessings with both Christians and non-Christians.[9]
- A leader should be able to demonstrate strong convictions and directness in taking a stand for righteousness, but to also balance these attitudes and actions with a loving spirit.[10]
- A vision-driven person.
- A person of integrity and honesty.
- A good manager of his or her own home (I Timothy 3:4).
- Not addicted to alcohol (I Timothy 3:3).
- Understands that God is his or her leader
- Not a drug-addict
- Good reputation in and out of the church community (I Timothy 3:7).
- He or she is hard working. There is no by-pass. There is no easy way to biblical leadership positions. The Blackabys write: "leadership is

[9] Barna, *Leaders on Leadership* , 91.
[10] Ibid, 98.

hard work. There are no shortcuts."[11]

- He or she has strong communication skills and knows how to communicate well with members as well as outsiders.

So, any true United Methodist who wants to be on the leadership team- called the church council- must possess the qualities that are put forth here and even more. These will help an individual to be the kind of leader God wants him or her to be.

Every true United Methodist leader must read, pray and meditate on this hymn Richard Baxter penned down years ago:

Lord, it belongs not to my care whether I die or live; to love and serve thee is my share, and this thy grace must give.

If life be long, I will be glad that I may long obey; if short, yet why should I be sad to soar to the endless day?

Christ leads me through no dark rooms than he went through before; he that into God's kingdom comes must enter by this door.

Come, Lord, when grace hath made me meet thy blessed face to see; for if thy work on earth be sweet, what will thy glory be?

My knowledge of that life is small; the eye of faith is dim; but 'tis enough that Christ knows all, and I shall be with him.

QUESTIONS FOR REFLECTION

1. **Discuss biblical leadership.**

2. **Name five qualities of a Christian leader.**

3. **Give three characteristics of a secular leader.**

---

[11] Henry & Richard Blackaby, *Spiritual Leadership* (Nashville: B & H Publishing Group, 2001), 158.

CHAPTER 2

A LOCAL UNITED METHODIST CHURCH AND ITS FUNCTIONS

This chapter focuses on the definition of a local Church and its functions within the context of the United Methodist tradition. The church is a gathered people under the lordship of Jesus Christ. A local church is considered as God's people who gather and worship in a particular location.[Source??}

- What a local United Methodist Church is

    - A local United Methodist church is a place where conversion takes place; and converts are turned into disciples.
    - It is the assembly of true believers under the lordship of Jesus the Christ.
    - "It is the redemptive fellowship in which

the Word of God is preached by persons divinely called and the sacraments administered according to Christ's own appointment"[12].

- It is a congregation of faithful people where the pure Word of God is preached, and the baptism and the Lord's Supper duly administered according to Christ's ordinance.[13]
- A group of "called out believers" who assemble in Jesus' name (Matthew 18:20).
- It is an assembly of individuals who confess Jesus as Lord and Savior and practice their faith through the Wesleyan tradition.

a. The Mission And Vision Statements Of A Local Church

Every local church must have vision and mission statements. The vision statement states the *vision* of the local congregation. Vision in its simplest form, is where the leader wants the church to be at some point in time [the next month, one year, three years to five years, ten years, etc.]. It may be short, medium or long. Duration is a flexible aspect of vision. It will affect the vision most as far as its completion is concerned. The shorter the duration, the faster the elements needed to achieve the vision must be tackled.

A Japanese proverb states: "vision without action is a day dream. Action without vision is a nightmare." This is where a congregation's *mission* comes in the picture. The mission statement describes the things that must be done to fulfill the vision.

---

[12] *The Book of Discipline of the United Methodist Church* (Nashville: The United Methodist Publishing House, 2012), 143.

[13] Nolan B. Harmon, *Understanding the United Methodist Church* (Nashville: Parthenon, 1988), 45.

Imagine a situation where a carpenter has the concept to build a table –vision. Once the visualization is over, he considers how to get it done. The tools and steps in getting that task accomplished will now be the mission.

Another example could be: the vision of a local church may be: "***Winning Men and Women to God's Kingdom***." How the church reaches out (personal evangelism, crusade, etc.) to win men and women to God's Kingdom is the mission.

The global United Methodist Church has a vision and that vision is ***"making disciples for the transformation of the world".*** How this is done is left with each annual conference, district conference and the local church. There are several ways the UMC goes about this, for instance, street evangelism, small groups, prison ministry, hospital ministry, social advocacy, conferencing, revivals, crusades, strong discipleship programs, fellowshipping, media ministry, tracts explosion, etc.

b. Functions of a Local United Methodist Church

Each local church was established with a purpose in mind. However, certain functions are implicit and each congregation knows and understand this.

The Church, which is the body of Christ, came into existence for worship, evangelism and witness, good works and fellowship and edification.[14] Any institution that does these things mentioned here is referred to as a church. Anything contrary, then it cannot be a church.

For instance, the body of Christ exists for several reasons; all of which could fall into one or the other of these three main reasons:

---

[14] Wilbur O'Donovan, Biblical Christianity in An African Perspective, 163-164.

i. True Worship

Worship is a direct link to God. It opens us up to the vastness of the God we serve, not just the gifts and blessings but also sacrifice and service. The more we worship God, the more in tune we become with God's plan for our lives.

This furthers us into the state where we can deliver 'more' in our service. It then becomes part of our responsibilities to encourage our flocks to build up a strong worship culture. We can and should be willing to aid in the process but ultimately, we should give them enough support to be able to worship God by themselves.

ii. Building Up of Believers

We have a responsibility to build our flocks/[believers] holistically. If we place too much emphasis in one aspect of their lives, we will be failing them equally as if we did not place any focus on any aspect of their lives. A good Shepard uses every opportunity to make the flock grow to its fullest potential. It is important to develop a habit of worship but so is having believers with strong faith.

iii. Evangelizing the Lost.

A part of our Christian responsibility is to win over lost souls. A church is a key place where people come in search for answers and guidance to redemption. As servants, we should keep an open mind and heart as we guide these lost souls. We can't afford to be judgmental and condescending. As shepherds, it is our responsibility to provide an environment that is safe enough for anyone to walk in and get the necessary help they need to make right their past. The church or local pastor has no power to win souls for the Lord; however, s/he has a duty to provide anyone seeking Christ and His redemption a chance to be saved.

The Christian Church believes in the concept of One Lord,

One Hope and One Christ. Despite this concept, the Christian church is divided into denominations based on people's faith and how they see things. While the general church exists for reason discussed above, the United Methodist Church is focused here.

In an expanded form, The United Methodist Church exists for the following:[15]

- To assist individuals submit their lives to Christ and to live daily for Jesus.
- To carry on holistic ministries in its vicinity.
- To conduct trainings, workshops, and seminars for its membership and leadership to enhance their spiritual maturity.
- To do ministry along with other churches.
- To make sure that its membership respect God's creation.
- To put into place programs of evangelism, nurture and witness for its membership.

Additionally, the church exists for:

- Biblical doctrine(right preaching of the Word)
- Proper use of the sacraments(Baptism and the Lord's Supper)
- Right use of church discipline
- Genuine worship
- Effective prayer
- Effective witness

[15] *The Book of Discipline of the United Methodist Church*, 143-144.

- Effective fellowship
- Biblical church government
- Spiritual power in ministry
- Personal holiness of life among members
- Care for the poor and needy
- Love for Christ
- Christians can join forces together to fight the power of darkness (Ephesians 6:12).

The Authority of the Church

The church which came into existence on the Day of Pentecost has been given authority to bring people to Christ and to fight against the forces of evil. Before his death, Jesus Christ said this:

> *"And I will give unto thee the keys of the kingdom of heaven: and whatsoever thou shall bind on earth shall be bound in heaven; and whatsoever thou shall loose on earth shall be loosed in heaven"* (Matthew 16:19).

The authority of the church is spiritual. Wilbur O'Donovan in his book, Biblical Christianity in African perspective, says that Christians have Christ's power. Because Christians have Christ's power, they can overcome the plans and tricks of Satan and his demonic forces. Based on Christ's power active in the life of the church, Christians have authority above all powers of darkness and principalities.

The church has spiritual and moral authority. Authority to bind and loose; this authority is spiritual.

QUESTIONS FOR REFLECTION

1. **Define a Local Church.**
2. **Name three functions of a Local Church.**
3. **What is the vision for the global UMC?**
4. **Write down the Mission and Vision Statements of your church.**

CHAPTER 3

THE PASTOR AND HIS/HER FUNCTIONS

This section of the manual focuses on: who a pastor is and the pastor's tasks. It deals with the meaning and work of a pastor from general perspective and zeroes in on the responsibilities of a pastoral leader in the United Methodist Church.

- Who is a Local Pastor?

Let us look at few definitions:

- An individual who has been called by God to be an under-shepherd. He/she is either ordained or licensed by the chief shepherd of his or her denomination.
- A person who has received the gift of preaching, teaching and shepherding; and has been assigned

to superintend the affairs of a local church.

- The spiritual and temporal care-giver of the members and leaders of a particular local church.

- A spiritual overseer of a local congregation.

- A person who has been called by God, ordained or commissioned or licensed, to do pastoral work: preaching the Gospel of Jesus the Christ, teaching the Scriptures, witnessing to non-Christians, visiting the sick, pre-marital and post-marital counseling, administering the sacraments.

In the United Methodist Church, a pastor is:

  - "An ordained elder, provisional deacon, or licensed person approved by the vote of the clergy members in full connection and may be appointed by the bishop to be in charge of a station, circuit, cooperative parish, extension ministry, ecumenical shared ministry, or to a church of another denomination, or on the staff of one such appointment."[16]

- A spiritual leader who preaches the Word of God and bring about spiritual upliftment and growth to members of the congregation.[17]

- Work of a United Methodist Church Pastor

In the simplest form, a pastor is one called to serve. Therefore, in one form, anyone can be a pastor. However, this does not represent the office of a pastor. In as much as we are all called to

---

[16] Ibid, 267.

[17] J. Lamark Cox, Sr., *Handbook for Conference, District and Local Church Leaders* (Georgia: SCP /Third World Literature Publishing House, 1994), 37.

serve, we are each called into a separate and or special ministry. Thus, being called to serve as a 'pastor', one has taken on the onus of an office, which requires more than the mere sacrifice of being called. It requires total submission to God's will; obedience and lots of dedication. The office

From the general viewpoint, a pastor is called to:

- Feed God's people who are under his or her pastoral leadership (I Peter 5:2).
- Proclaim the whole will of God to all of God's people (Acts 20:27).
- Present every Christian under his or her care perfect in Christ Jesus (2 Cor. 11:3).
- Prepare every child of God for works of service (Ephesians 4:12).
- Equip every believer to evangelize (John 10:16).
- Carry on pre-marital and post-marital counseling.
- Superintend every ministry of the local congregation.
- Must love people
- Be in close communication with God
- Be a good listener

In the United Methodist Church, a pastor's role is summed up into four areas: Word and Ecclesial Acts, Sacrament, Order and Service. This means the pastor has a fourfold ministry.

See the expansion of the fourfold ministry that each pastor has to practice to experience transformation in a local church.

Word and Ecclesial Acts[18]*:*

In the United Methodist Church system, the entire faith is based upon the Word of God. Nothing is more important that what God instructs us to do or wants us to do

- To preach God's Word, direct worship; reader and teacher of the scriptures, and help the membership to study and to witness to their faith.

- To counsel individuals with "personal, ethical, or spiritual struggles".

- To conduct marriages and funerals.

- To pay regular visits especially among the sick and shut in, aged, imprisoned, and the needy.

- To be a person of confidentiality. Keep people's secrets except in cases where mandatory reporting is required by the law.

Sacraments[19:]

From the United Methodist background, sacraments are "symbols and pledges of the Christian's profession and God's love toward us. They are means of God's grace by which God works invisibly in us, quickening, strengthening and confirming our faith in him."

United Methodists believe in two sacraments. They are *Baptism* and the *Lord's Supper*. People of the Methodist faith believe that these were practiced by Lord Jesus.

---

[18] *The Book of Discipline of the United Methodist Church,* 267-268.
[19] Ibid, 268.

United Methodists believe that baptism "signifies entrance into the household of faith, and is a symbol of repentance and inner cleansing from, a representation of the new birth in Christ Jesus and a mark of Christian discipleship."

We, United Methodists, are convinced that the Lord's Supper is a "representation of our redemption, a memorial of the sufferings and death of Christ, and a token of love and union which Christians have with Christ and with one another."

Thus, United Methodist pastors do the following under the sacraments:

- Carry on the sacraments of Baptism and the Lord's Supper
- "To encourage the private and congregational use of the other means of grace."

Order[20]*:*

For the United Methodist Church, when we talk about order, the focus is on providing leadership for the local church. It talks about leading in administrative matters, financial matters and other ministry matters. Below are functions that the pastors carry out under order as a part of the fourfold ministry:

- Serves as the Chief Executive Officer (administrative officer) of the local congregation and makes sure that the church functions well.
- Conducts the temporal affairs of the local church.

---

[20] Ibid, 269.

- Be a part of the UMC programs and take advantage of training opportunities provided by the district or annual conference.

- Encourages the congregation members to accept one another irrespective of racial, social and ethnic backgrounds.

Service[21]*:*

As a part of the fourfold ministry of the pastors, service is an essential component of the pastoral ministry. Service has to do with helping the local church to do things that the touch the lives of people.

- To incorporate the teachings of Christ Jesus in "servant ministries and servant leadership."

- To help the church to be discipleship -based.

- To help the church to be a giving and caring community.

- Some Restrictions on a United Methodist Pastor22:

    - No pastor is allowed to organize a local church without the consent of the bishop.

    - No pastor shall leave his or her assignment between sessions of the annual conference without the consent of the district superintendent and or the bishop.

---

[21] Ibid, 270.

[22] Ibid, 270-271.

- No pastor should conduct any marriage ceremonies that bring homosexuals in union.
- No pastor is to practice re-baptism. The Wesleyan tradition does not support this act.
- No pastor is to conduct any worship service at a local church that he or she is not assigned without the consent of the pastor-in-charge.

QUESTIONS FOR REFLECTION

1. **WHO IS A PASTOR?**
2. **DISCUSS AT LEAST THREE FUNCTIONS OF A PASTOR.**

CHAPTER 4

UNDERSTANDING THE DIVERSITIES OF CONGREGATIONS

God created the human race to worship him (Isaiah 43:7). The Prophet Isaiah says in Isaiah 43:9: "Let all the nations be gathered and let the peoples be assembled."

This acknowledges the fact that God desires us to praise and worship him.

People who have come to faith in Yahweh gather in places to give adoration to their Creator. Such gathering is referred to as congregation.

Congregations are diverse. This section will deal with the definition of congregation, the essence of gathering congregating, what attracts people to congregations,

congregations in the old and New Testament periods, contemporary look at congregations, types of congregations, and the pastor as the pacesetter of the congregation.

Congregation Defined

Congregation is widely used in the Christian gatherings as well as other religious gatherings. It is the assembling of people who gather to pay allegiance to a supreme being through the acts of worship, nurture and witnessing. To further expand on this in the context of Christianity, it is a gathered people in a locale who exercise their faith in Jesus, the Christ as their personal Savior and at the same time focus on worship, edification and witnessing.

James F. Hopewell defines congregation as "a specific and available instance of human society expressed in symbolic activities that grasp society's plight and hope".[23]

From The United Methodist viewpoint, a congregation is seen as a local church. And a local church is, "the redemptive fellowship in which the Word of God is preached by persons divinely called and the sacraments are duly administered according to Christ's own appointment. And it exists for the maintenance of worship, the edification of believers, and the redemption of the world."[24]

The Essence of Congregating

The Bible requires that Christians congregate. The writer of Hebrews says: "Let us not give up meeting together, as some are

---

[23] James F. Hopewell, *Congregation –Stories and Structures* (Philadelphia: Fortress Press, 1987), 12.

[24] *The Book of Discipline of the United Methodist Church* (Nashville: The United Methodist Publishing House, 2012), 143.

in the habit of doing, but let us encourage one another – and the more as you see the Day approaching"(Hebrews 10:25, NIV). In this text, people gather in congregations to encourage one another as they worship the Lord.

God understands the need to form bonds that bind and build our faith. As individuals we are prone to fall but with the power of number, any such failures may be reduced to a manageable level. Thus, as we congregate, we are encouraged and our faith is strengthened. We get the extra bread we may need from the greater whole. This does not mean that we will never fail or sin. It simply presents us an opportunity to be helped by people who have gone through the experience. Because there is power in numbers, it sometimes become comforting and secure.

Besides the above, individuals have different reasons for gathering. No gathering or assembly is held without a purpose in mind. Therefore, people come to a local church for different reasons. Since all congregants do not attend worship services for the same reasons, leaders need to create an environment of safety for the most number of congregants. The wider this safety net is, the better the chance for such congregations to achieve its full potential.

For example, some people congregate to worship and to remember together.[25]

Some also gather to express their religious experience in the larger world.

Further, the author of Clay Jars states that people gathered to worship the Lord Jesus the Christ for the following reasons: "have an oasis of peacefulness and rest amidst a hectic life. Get inspired and lifted up; and receive practical advice from the sermon that can be applied during the week."[26]

---

[25] C. Ellis Nelson, *Congregations: Their Power to Form and Transform* (Atlanta: John Knox Press, 1988), 71.

[26] George Thompson, Jr., Treasures In Clay Jars: New Ways To Understand Your Church (Eugene: Wipf and Stock Publishers, 2003), 71.

Others come to the church to meet with their dates. Still others do come because they have an appointment with a church member. Some do come to worship services because it is a place where they can enrich themselves. People come to see and to be seen.

Congregations exist to "serve people, not the other way around."[27] Weems and Michel say, "A deep concern for the plight of people and a desire to help people should be a common bond for a new generation and the link that binds the church with those outside the church who are deeply concerned about helping others".[28] The congregation has the responsibility to also serve midlife members as well.

In serving them, special programs should be put into place to meet their needs. The midlife congregations are individuals in the congregation between the ages 35 and 55. They too can have "rich time of exploration, growth and discovery"[29] in the congregation.

Christ the Savior of the human race came to earth to serve humanity (Matthew 20:28; Philippians 2:7). He did not come for the human race to serve him. Each congregation has that responsibility to serve its members and outsiders. Christ was called to service so is the Church today.

The Spirit of the Lord has been released to assist the human race in service (John 14:25-27). The Holy Spirit comes alongside us Christians to do the work of ministry. The congregations are empowered by the Holy Spirit to carry on the work of ministry. Simply put, servant leadership is a key component of the ministry of the congregation.

---

[27] Lovett W. Weems & Anna A. Michel. *The Crisis of Young Clergy*(Nashville: Abingdon Press,2008) , 106.
[28] Ibid., 106.
[29] Lynne M. Baab, *Embracing Midlife Congregations as Support Systems* (Virginia: Alban Institute Publication, 1999), 36.

The Forces that Attract People to Congregations

While on one of his ministry journeys, the crowd followed Jesus. And this is what Jesus said: "I tell you the truth, you are looking for me not because you saw miraculous signs but because you ate the loaves and had your fill."(John 6:26, NIV). This implies that they followed Jesus the Christ for several reasons. So, it is with businesses and the congregations.

Every business does a lot of advertisement to draw people's attention. Businesses do attract many customers. Customers care is paramount for most businesses. The same concept applies with congregations. Thompson declares, "religion operates in a marketplace, where consumers select churches based on how well their emphases and activities meet the particular consumer's identified needs".[30]

What the writer tries to note here is applicable to the greater body polity of religion. People are concerned about miracles, healing and deliverance, so they move to churches that have the ability to speak to their needs. When the people desire to worship God in a specific way, they find the congregations that appeal to their needs.

People are attracted to churches based on warm fellowship, the kind of worship, the kind of messages that are preached and the kind of ministry activities that are carried out in the congregation. For example, inspiring sermons draw people's attention to a congregation. Others do come to the congregation "because friends or relatives invited them. There is nothing new about this approach. It began when Andrew introduced Simon to Jesus, and it has carried the Christian faith from generation to generation for twenty centuries."[31]

---

[30] George Thompson, Jr., Treasures *In Clay Jars: New Ways To Understand Your Church* (Eugene: Wipf and Stock Publishers, 2003), 71.

[31] Boyce A. Bowdon, S*elling Your Church in the '90s- A Public Relations Guide for Clergy and Laity* (Oklahoma: Koinonia Press,1992), 42.

Another thing that attracts people to a congregation is the congregation's image. The way people perceive the church to be is important. Thus, every congregation should strive to have a good image. Jesus was also concerned about image. "He was egomaniac, preoccupied with polls. Jesus cared about his image because he knew that people's perceptions of him would influence their response."[32]

The hard truth is that we live in a world where image plays a critical role in the choices we make, we will make, and those we are currently making.

Our congregants will apply similar logic when selecting which church they fellowship with at any given point in time. Even that decision to select our congregation will be predicated upon several other factors, most of which we as leaders will be directly responsible. To keep members, we constantly need to make choices that affect our image positively.

Congregations in the Old Testament Period

Everything has a source. For people to gather and worship a supreme being commenced from somewhere. The assembling of people did not start in the eighteenth century.

The people of Israel were referred to as a congregation at the time of Moses. The Lord put into place an arrangement where the people would be ruled by him. That is, the theocratic form of governance (Exodus 19:3-9; 24:6-8). The Israelites were asked to gather at the tent to worship God (Exodus 25:8-9; 33:7-11). The Tent of Meeting was a place set apart for worship. It was a place where sacrifices were made unto the Lord.

---

[32] Ibid., 51.

Congregations in the New Testament Period

Congregations in the New Testament period are quite different from ours today. The early church which we can also refer to as "congregation" met in the homes of individuals (Romans 16:3-5; I Corinthians 16:9; Colossians 4:15; Philemon 1:1-2). The church did not own a house to be called a church building. There was no official church building until A.D. 232.[33]

The church was born on the Day of Pentecost. People did not worship in gigantic buildings that we have nowadays. Though the congregation did not worship in beautiful edifices as we have today, the church grew explosively in the early days.

Jesus Christ was worshipped in a house-church (Matthew 2:11). The home of Peter the Apostle was used as a meeting place for healing services (Matthew 8:14-16). Again, the first communion service was held in a house (Matthew 26:18). Bob Fitts in his book *The House Church: The New Testament Model For Model for Multiplying Congregations says:*

Our Lord could have chosen to celebrate the first communion with His disciples in a synagogue, in the Temple, or in some other place of religious importance. However, he chose to celebrate it in a common, ordinary house in accordance with the Jewish custom of Passover. Thus, He set his approval on the common dwelling place as a holy and sanctified place. It was worthy of the most solemn worship services.[34]

The house-church congregations played an important role in the Kingdom of God. Here are some key things that occurred in the House-church:

The first worship service happened in a house. The first communion service was in a house. The first healing service was

---

[33] Bob Fitts, Sr., Acts -*The House Church: The New Testament Model for Multiplying Congregations*, Volume 30, no.2 (April/May/June 2002), 2.
[34] Ibid., 6.

conducted in a house. The first instance of the preaching of the Gospel to the Gentiles came about in the house of Cornelius. The outpouring of the Holy Spirit on the day of Pentecost was in a house, and the first churches that the Apostle Paul planted were all organized in houses. Lydia's house was Europe's first church.[35]

Congregations in Contemporary Times

Today, the church is housed in small, medium and large buildings of its own. These huge edifices around our globe also started as house-churches. The present day churches have huge attendances than the gatherings in the New Testament time. In addition, these churches or congregations are not seen just as people who gathered to worship, build each other and witness. Human beings are considered social beings. Therefore, in dealing with the congregations, individuals should not see the church from only the spiritual or supernatural level. Their social make-up must also be considered.

As spiritual leaders, we need to make conscious efforts to be sensitive to the diversity of our congregation. It is often tempting to leave out some classes of people or place more emphasis on another group. We may base this on social standings in society but we should guide against it.

In his book, *How To Get Along with Your Church*, George Thompson focuses on how the pastors can get along with the people they have come to work with, in their ministries. For him the church has something that the pastor can use to make headway in doing the work of ministry. Each local congregation has landmines.

---

[35] Ibid., 6-7.

Therefore, every pastor must be mindful about the landmines of the congregation he or she is assigned to manage. The landmines[36] include levels of culture, layers of culture, and cultural confluence.

Moving from one charge to another, the pastor will experience different ways of approaching the landmines of the congregations she or he gets to work with. George Thompson says this about the pastors who take a new assignment: "a new pastor does not build cultural capital by behaving in ways that dishonor the church's own culture."[37]

Nancy Ammerman, looking at congregations, suggests that individuals see congregations from various spectra of life[38]: theology, ecology, culture, resources, dynamics of congregational life, and leadership.

She also states that doing a careful analysis of congregations is very crucial. She puts forth the following as methods of studying congregations[39]: direct observation, interview, congregational timeline, archival document analysis, and questionnaires and surveys.

Types of Congregations

There are different congregations in the Liberia Annual Conference of the United Methodist Church. Some of the churches are affluent, potential while others are struggling for survival as they carry out ministries.

---

[36] Thompson, *How To Get Along With Your Church-Creating Cultural Capital for Doing Ministry*, 1-26.
[37] Ibid., 23.
[38] Ammerman, *Studying Congregations – A New Handbook*, 23-29.
[39] Ibid.,196-238.

Homogeneous Congregations

Homogeneous congregations are congregations that are very unique from other congregations. In these congregations, worshippers belong to one ethnic group. These congregations have one common heritage.

For example, there are homogenous congregations in the United Methodist Church in Liberia. For instance, the Faith United Methodist Church on the Monrovia District Conference is a Kpelle Congregation.

Heterogeneous Congregations

Heterogeneous congregations are congregations with people from different language backgrounds. These congregations have different age groupings. Moreover, people have different kind of educational backgrounds as well as different social statuses. For instance, the First United Methodist Church of the Monrovia District Conference of the Liberia Annual Conference is a church that is heterogeneous.

In this church, there are Americo-Liberians as well as indigenous Liberians.

The congregants come together to worship irrespective of their economic, social, ethnic, and educational backgrounds. Such congregations have their own intricacies.

Heterogeneous congregations use different forms of worship to please the congregants. Multiple types of worship are experienced in such congregations. Ministers of the gospel have many challenges in dealing with such congregations.

Poorer (Struggling) Congregations

In the Liberia Annual Conference, some churches are economically struggling. Such churches do not have the capacity to carry out ministry effectively and efficiently because of the lack of financial resources.

Sometimes, these churches also lack the human resource – those who have the capacity to plan and take the ministry of the church to the next level. It may surprise you that some of those churches are found in the urban areas of Liberia.

For example, the Faith United Methodist Church of the Monrovia District Conference cannot afford to pay its pastor as well as meeting up with her apportionment to the Monrovia District Conference. For two years, this congregation has not been present at district conference. Few years ago, this same church could not send her pastor to the 180th Annual Session of the Liberia Annual Conference of the United Methodist Church for lack of funds.[40]

If this is happening in Monrovia, it means the churches in the rural parts have their own experiences. There are several districts of the Liberia Annual Conference, which have churches, or congregations that are struggling to carry out the gospel. In one of the districts in eastern Liberia, pastors receive coconuts as their salaries and benefits. They do not receive cash as it is in other parts of the country. The Bishop of the Liberia Annual Conference, the United Methodist Church, Bishop John G. Innis, announced at the 179th Annual Session of the Liberia Annual Conference that the pastors were making many sacrifices for the sake of the gospel. He informed leaders and members of the Conference that such pastors need special attention.

---

[40] This information was given at the last 162nd Annual Session of the Monrovia District Conference of the Liberia Annual Conference that took place in December 2012 at the S.T. Nagbe United Methodist church , Sinkor, Monrovia.

In such a congregation, the pastors have to do extra- curricular activities to earn something for the survival of the family. In the rural areas, such pastors get heavily engaged into subsistence farming to feed their families and meet some other basic needs.

Such congregations cannot grow spiritually because the focus is not there. No money syndrome takes over such a congregation. Therefore, a minister from a struggling church cannot administer the same way he or she administers in a potential as well as the wealthy congregation.

Middle Class (Potential) Congregations

These are congregations in the Liberia Annual Conference that are not well-to-do but have the potential to carry out different ministry activities. They have the ability to pay their pastors salary and other benefits. These congregations have all sorts of people as well. In these congregations, the rich, the poor, and the needy are available.

These congregations find themselves at the midpoint. They have the potential to pay pastors and other church workers.

Wealthy (Well-to-do) Congregations

These are congregations, which have the full potential to take care of the ministry activities of the congregations. They may not be wealthy as the wealthiest churches in America and Europe. These churches are able to meet some of the basic needs of their members, regular visitors and others. These congregations afford parsonages and vehicles for ministry.

The First United Methodist Church of Monrovia is one of the rich congregations in the Liberia Annual Conference. This church has real estate properties, well-to-do members and top business executives as well as top government officials do. It also has huge monthly budget for salaries and benefits for more than thirty staff persons. Its monthly salaries and benefits budget is around Ten Thousand United States Dollars.[41]

As an abled church, the First United Methodist Church is involved with many outreach activities. This church built a new edifice for the Peter Jeru United Methodist Church of the Kakata/Farmington River District Conference of the Liberia Annual Conference. Thereafter, the Church built an elementary school, which is located in Siaffa-keh Town, Grand Cape Mount County. This school is in the St. Paul River District Conference of the Liberia Annual Conference.

Another church is the Stephen Trowen Nagbe United Methodist Church. This church is the second wealthiest church in the Liberia Annual Conference. Its apportionment to the Monrovia District Conference and the Liberia Annual Conference is the second highest.[42] It constructed another church edifice in the Weala District Conference.

Wealthy churches have economic power to reach out to do many ministry works. They also have the human resources to carry out the kind of ministries they desire to implement. In these congregations, there a lot of things put into place to get the various ministries ongoing. Their hands are always open and the hearts are prepared to touch the lives of people.

Missional Congregations[43]

Congregations are not just poor, rich and potential. They are also missional congregations. Missional congregations focus on the Great Commission of Jesus Christ that is recorded in the Gospels and the epistles. A missional church does a lot in

---

[41] This information comes from the salary and benefits budget for the month of May, 2013. This information was provided by William Boayou, the Finance Officer of the First United Methodist Church.

[42] This information is in the Monrovia District Conference 2013 Budget.

[43] Nelson, *Congregations Their Power to from and Transform*, 88.

planting new churches. It moves by expanding the Kingdom of God where the gospel has not reached. Church planting is a high priority for a missional congregation. Making disciples becomes the primary concern for every church that is called the church of Jesus the Christ.

This is the command the missional congregation follows: "Go ye therefore, and teach all nations, baptizing them in the name of the Father, and of the Son, and of the Holy Ghost:

Teaching them to observe all things whatsoever I have commanded you: and, lo, I am with you always, even unto the end of the world" (Matthew 28:19-20, KJV). This type of congregation plants churches where the Lord directs. It plants churches in virgin territories.[44]

An African Christian medical doctor and evangelist, Dag Heward-Mills declares that a missional church is a church that has the mind of Christ. The preacher writes that having the mind of Christ involves understanding that God is monitoring our works; church planting is the key to going all the way with God; you are expected to accomplish certain works whilst on earth; and the strength of a church is measured by its sending capacity.[45]

The Congregation as a Social Entity

The Christian church is not just about teaching people about heavenly matters. The physical as well as the social life of the congregants must be taken into consideration. Christians are social beings.

---

[44] Dag Heward Mills, *Church Planting* (Wellington: Lux Verbi BM (Pty) Ltd, 2008), 5.
[45] Ibid, 8-22.

The church must be holistic in carrying out its responsibilities. It should take into consideration every aspect of its membership: family life, employment and health needs.

In our part of the world, too much emphasis is made on people developing a better relationship with their Creator and forgetting to look at the social life of the people.

Every Local Congregation Is Not The Same

There are five hundred ninety-seven churches[46] in the Liberia Annual Conference. Even though these churches are Methodist in doctrine and practice, yet they carry on ministries in different ways. Three areas are considered here: worship (music), Communion (the Lord's Supper) and giving (plate offering).

In the area of music, the First UMC of the Monrovia District Conference uses western music in its worship services. Hymns are sung in English. The organists and choristers play and sing respectively in English. At the Trinity UMC also in the Monrovia District, all the music is sung in a traditional language called Kru. All western songs are put into the traditional language. In the Saint Paul River District, the Eddie Memorial UMC does its music in English while the Jeru UMC in the Kakata/Farmington River District does its music in the Bassa language.

In administering the Lord's Supper, every local United Methodist Congregation does it differently. For the First UMC in Monrovia, only the pastors administer the Lord's Supper; no lay person. In addition, the communicants kneel to take the bread and wine. At the New Georgia UMC, some of the communicants do kneel while others stand. Laypersons aid the

---

[46] This information is taken from the 2011 Journal of the 178th Session of the Liberia Annual Conference of the United Methodist Churc,pp.237-262

pastors in the administration of the Lord's Supper. At the E.J. Goodridge UMC of the St. Paul River District, communicants stand to take the Lord's Supper. And at the First UMC in the Grand Bassa District, communicants stand to take the communion elements.

Considering giving, at the First UMC in Monrovia, members sit in their seats while the offering plates are passed around. At the Wesley UMC in Kakata/Farmington River District and the E. Jonathan Goodridge UMC of the St. Paul River District, members move to the front while singing and dancing to put their offerings into the boxes.

Different People in Local Congregations

Each congregation in the United Methodist Church in Liberia has different people. There are youths, young adults, men, children and women in the churches. There are lay people and the clergy. In each congregation, rich people, poor people, government officials, business people, the middle class as well as the upper class are found. Additionally, people are at different levels in their spiritual sojourn.

Each local church has people who are highly educated while others are not educated. Some people speak their local languages while others do not have any local language to speak.

Still other local congregations have people from different nationalities who attend worship services. For example, the First UMC in Monrovia has Ghanaians, Nigerians, and Filipinos worshipping at the church.

Every congregation does operate in a different manner. This means that every local church has different ways of worshipping. The ways the local church operates is its culture. So, the minister has a key role to play in taking that local congregation to another level. He or she must carry on a study of the congregation.

The Pastor As The Pacesetter of the Congregation

Understanding the culture of a congregation is very important for the pastor to carry on effective and efficient ministry. The Lord Jesus commissioned the disciples to move out to tell the dying world about God's kingdom principles. As he sent them out, Jesus told his men not to venture into the gentile territories for they had not yet understood the cultural intricacies of the Gentiles (Matthew 10:1-6). The disciples went into the terrains and the people they knew already. Therefore the pastor must take the following into consideration:

Know the Congregation[47]

The pastor must know the people. He/she is doing ministry with the people and not for the people. Knowing the people will help the minister identify the kind of people that make up the congregation.

There are members who are faithful, available and teachable (FAT) Christians. The pastor's acquaintance with his or her members will aid him or her to identify and know the traits of the members – knowing those who are slow, quick, easy going, "frogs"[48] and "snails"[49].

---

[47] Thompson, *How to Get Along Your Church- Creating Cultural Capital for Doing Ministry*, 91.

[48] At a Leadership workshop held with the Gompa District Conference of the Liberia Annual Conference of the United Methodist Church, some of the participants said that some members in the churches behave like frogs – this means there are congregants who make a lot of noise – the noisy people.

[49] Those members who are referred to as "snails" are members who are very slow. Snails are very slow in movement.

Leadership plays a key role in the Christian church. As one leads, the followers have key interest to find out whether that leader is concerned about the people.

John Maxwell says "people will never care how much you know until they know how much you care for them. The pastors have the responsibility to show care and concern for the members[50].

In knowing the congregation, the pastor must also get to know the tribal leader[51]. No pastor should do ministry in a new local church without "seeking counsel with the tribal leader."[52] Relationship building between the pastor and key leaders is essential for ministry.

Additionally, leadership is about building relationship. "A leader is not a leader unless other people are involved."[53] A leader must have a following. He or she needs people to carry out the work of the ministry.

Knowing the people in the congregation is a helpful tool for effective and efficient ministry. This will aid the pastor in identifying their spiritual journeys[54] of his or her members. Individuals are at different levels in their walk with the Lord.

Some people are just at the beginning of the spiritual journey. Some are far ahead in their relationship with the Lord. Some are in the congregation yet they do not have personal relationship with the Lord.

---

[50] John Maxwell, *Developing the Leader Within You* (Nashville: Thomas Nelson, Inc., 1993), 3.

[51] The tribal leader is the holder of the church's culture. This person is also the connecting point.

[52] Robert C. Anderson, *The Effective Pastor: A Practical Guide to Ministry* (Chicago: Moody Press,1998), 110.

[53] George M. Hillman, Jr., *Ministry Greenhouse: Cultivating Environments for Practical Learning* (Virginia: The Alban Institute, 2008), 76.

[54] W. James Cowell, *Incorporating New Members: Bonds of Believing, Belonging, and Becoming* (Nashville: Discipleship Resources, 1992), 6-7.

Appreciate People

A pastor who wants to make a difference in his or her ministry should make it his or her business to appreciate people. Appreciating members of the congregation is a springboard for the people to begin to trust the pastor. Carl S. Dudley and his colleagues say:

"Before a pastor can be trusted to identify changes or developments that are appropriate and possible for those who compose the churches in culture, he or she must appreciate them."[55]

Every leadership should concentrate on the people. Here is a statement from Malcolm Warford: "Leadership centers in the care of the people who make up an organization and the mission of the organization itself."[56]

Leaders should show appreciation by expressing thanks to their members for their participation in activities in the congregation. Send members thank-you cards.

Ability to Listen[57]

The pastor will accomplish a lot if s/he does more listening than talking. A listening ear will get more than a talking mouth. Listening helps the minister to hear more he or she needs to hear.

Paying attention to people matters a lot than speaking thousands of stuff that will not help touch the core of ministry the Lord has called you to.

---

[55] Carl S. Dudley et al, *Carriers of Faith: Lessons from Congregational Studies* (Louisville: Westminster/John Knox Press, 1991), 149.

[56] Malcolm Warford, *Becoming A New Church-Reflections on Faith and Calling* (Ohio: United Church Press, 2000), 98.

[57] Thompson, Jr., *How to Get Along with Your Church- Creating Cultural Capital for Doing Ministry*, 53.

George Thompson writes this in his book: "If you are appointed to the church, you have had to listen carefully right away, in order to begin identifying the congregation's values.[58]

People will draw closer to people who take time to listen to them. Some leaders want to do all the talking and do little listening. This is not a good practice for anyone who is in leadership.

Dag Heward-Mills declares: "Learn the art of listening rather than talking. When you allow people to talk about themselves they psychologically feel that they are closer to you. This makes them rally around you."[59]

Grace to Adapt[60]

If the pastor will want to make impact and leave an imprint on the minds of the people, the pastor may have to accept some stuff and see how he or she and the congregation can move forward. Adaptation does not mean that one participates in all that is being practiced by the congregation.

The Apostle Paul declares: "To the weak became I as weak, that I might gain the weak: I am made all things to all [men], that I might by all means save some" (I Corinthians 9:22).

This is a good principle that the Apostle Paul lived out which led him to make great impact in the Christian community during his lifetime.

---

[58] Ibid., 53.

[59] Dag Heward-Mills, *The Art of Leadership* (Accra: Parchment House, 2003), 54.

[60] Thompson, Jr. , *How to get along with your church- Creating Cultural Capital for Doing Ministry* , 43.

Capacity to Learn[61]

Nobody knows everything. God is the only one who is omniscient.

Not every area of work is the same. There are different ways people carry out their operations. Therefore, no minister of the gospel should be too big to learn. Learning is very important for any leader who wants to grow and take his or people to the next level. It gives you the opportunity to think and rethink the task that has been entrusted to you care. Thinking and rethinking will help the pastor make informed and sound decisions in the ministry.

Jack Welch also acknowledges that learning is very important. Leaders should not stop learning. This is what Welch writes: "keep learning: Don't be arrogant, he insists. Don't assume you know it all. Always assume that you can learn from someone else.[62]

A leader must be someone who is willing to learn to make sure that his or her ministry moves forward. Learning leads to embracing new ideas for the work of ministry.

A Ghanaian evangelist and writer declares:

> Your leadership will be stunted if you are not prepared to embrace new ideas. The world is constantly changing. Old systems and approaches no longer work. Computers have refashioned the way we do things. Seasons change. Needs change. And people change. That is why God constantly introduces fresh and new things. God is a God of change.[63]

---

[61] Ibid, 53.

[62] Robert Slater, *29 Leadership Secrets from Jack Welch(* McGraw-Hill : New York, 2003), 50.

[63] Dag Heward-Mills, *The Successful Leader*(Accra: Parchment House, 2002), 40-41.

Pastoral leadership should make sure to learn new things. The world is changing. The pastor must have the grace to learn. Learning provides the opportunity to see new things and hear new things. No leader should close his or her life to the process of learning. Leaders are called to always be learners. Learners do grow. So, pastors should grow through the process of learning. The Pastor must "treat every new assignment as a start-over, even if it is not."[64]

Learning is a good practice that enhances a pastor's ministry. It opens the doors to get the congregational identity[65]: its history, rituals, beliefs, values, artifacts, stories, myths, ways of dealing with visitors, and other factors that distinguish one congregation from others. Paul reminds us to "Do your best to present yourself to God as approved, a workman who does not need to be ashamed and who correctly handles the word of truth"(II Tim. 2:15, NIV).

Be A Team Player

Team playing is very important in doing ministry. The pastor alone cannot do everything. Jesus was a great team player. He was not an independent operator but was accountable to and under the authority of his Father (John 5:19). Several persons did ministry in team[66]: Barnabas, Saul and John Mark (Acts13:4-13), Paul, Barnabas, Judas and Silas (Acts 15:22-43), Paul and Silas (Acts 15:36-41), and Paul Silas, Luke and Timothy (Acts 16:1-17:34).

---

[64] Kouzes , James M. and Barry Z. Posner, *The Leadership Challenge* (San Francisco: Jossey-Bass Publishers, 1995), 61.

[65] Matthew Floding, *Welcome To Theological Field Education* (Virginia: The Alban Institute, 2011), 79.

[66] Justin Dennison, *Team Ministry: A Blueprint for Christian Leadership* (Great Britain: OM Books, 1997), 22-24.

Team playing is the "ability for people to participate whether children, youths, or adults in the whole of the congregation, not just the parts."[67]

The following are seen in team playing: "complementing gifts, ministry strengths, gift development, support system, intensified vision and greater productivity."[68] A pastor needs others to effect meaningful changes in the congregation.

The Source of Congregating

God, the Creator of the universe is the foundation of congregations. He likes people to assemble. Several times, the Lord requested the children of Israel to assemble. Jesus himself assembled many people to share the good news about the Kingdom of God.

Even in contemporary time, people do still assemble. The Bible says in Hebrews 10:25 that believers should not neglect the assembly of believers.

Conclusion

God created the universe. Everything that has been created has its source in God. Therefore, culture is a part of God's creative acts (Genesis 1:26-2:15). Human beings were given the mandate to develop the earth. The process of tilling the earth and procreation signify the beginning of culture. It is "not independent of the Godhead".[69]

---

[67] Kennon L. Callahan, *Small, Strong Congregations-Creating Strengths and Health for Your Congregation* (San Francisco: Jossey-Bass, 2000), 192.

[68] Ibid., 33-34.

[69] Malphurs, *Look Before You Lead: How To Discern and Shape Your church Culture*, 23.

Every congregation has its own culture. The culture is very important for a local congregation. It is the life of the individuals who make up the membership of the church. It is sometimes considered the bloodline of the people who belong to a specific congregation.

QUESTIONS FOR REFLECTION

1. **Discuss the essence for congregating.**

2. **What is a congregation?**

3. **Why should the pastor be the pace setter of a local congregation?**

CHAPTER 5

WHO BECOMES A MEMBER ON THE LEADERSHIP TEAM IN A LOCAL CHURCH?

The leadership team in a local UMC is the church council. To desire to serve on the council is something good; and worth encouraging. But the truth here is that everyone cannot serve on the council. You may want to ask why. You see, holding a leadership position in a local church is quite different from holding a position in any social institution.

To discuss who holds a position on the church council, it is important to talk a little about membership in a local United Methodist Church. In any local UMC, the membership is divided into categories: full membership, affiliate membership, associate membership and preparatory membership.

Full Membership

Professing members are those who hold membership in a particular local church through the profession of faith in Christ. Transferred persons who held full membership in the churches they are transferred from falls in this category also.

Affiliate Membership

Affiliate members are those who hold membership in another local United Methodist Church but worshipping at another local UMC away from their home churches. Watch-care members fall in this category.

Associate Membership

Associate members are Christians from other denominations who are worshipping at a local United Methodist away from their home churches. They have their own reasons worshipping at the church.

Preparatory Membership

Preparatory Members are recent converts who are undergoing preparation in the church's membership class; and children who are baptized and are yet to become full members. The children are confirmed at the age of consent – can begin from maybe at 12 years old.

Holding a position in a local United Methodist Church is important. The United Methodist Church is a Christian church; and it follows the principles of the Holy Bible. Those who should be given leadership positions are those who are in full membership in the local congregation.

In addition, positions should be given to members who have been adequately disciple and are mature in the Christian faith.

Let us look at what Paul told Timothy: **"and the things you have heard me say in the presence of many witnesses entrust to reliable men who will also be qualified to teach others."**

Therefore, to take leadership position, one must be a professing member. Novices in Christiany should not be given leadership position in the church. The leadership and development committee must recruit leaders for the church based on biblical leadership principles.

QUESTIONS FOR REFLECTION

1. **NAME THE CATEGORIES OF MEMBERSHIP IN A LOCAL CHURCH.**
2. **WHO IS A FULL MEMBER OF A LOCAL CHURCH?**
3. **EXPLAIN ASSOCIATE AND AFFILIATE MEMBERSHIPS.**

CHAPTER 6

THE LOCAL CHURCH COUNCIL AND ITS FUNCTIONS

An executive body and a set of rules govern every organization. For the local United Methodist church, it is the Church Council. This is the highest decision making body in any local church, specifically in regards to administrative matters on the overall administration of the church.

It functions like most other boards in the circular world. The local pastor remains the administrative and spiritual head of the church s/he is assigned.

Whilst the board concerns itself with the overall short to long-term growth of the church, the pastor deals with the immediate, every day aspects of the church- more like the CEO does.

a. The Purpose of the Church Council

As noted above, the Church Council [Administrative Board/Council] has the generic oversight responsibility of the church. It is made up of the leader of every sub-arm in the church- youth, young adult, women, men usher, etc.].

The general idea here is that the individual parts come together and form a whole that should be greater. Information flow in the UMC church is mostly top to bottom. When the board meets, it makes decisions, which are then taken down to its various arms by the leaders who helped to make that decision. These leaders also take information up the chain.

Theoretically, this process should be smooth but the complexity of human nature prevents it from being this way.

Decisions on the other hand are not just top to bottom as is the case with information. When an arm of the church meets, it runs based on the structure it is designed to follow. They then take that decision upward the chain through its leader who presents it to the Council for approval where necessary. This degree of liberty allows for the smooth running of the church. Thus, decisions are made both top to bottom and bottom to top.

The church council exists for the following purposes[70]:

- Plans and carries out the programs of nurture, outreach, witness and resources.
- Evaluates the mission and ministry of the local church
- Administers the church's organization and temporal life
- The visionary arm of the local church

[70] Book of Discipline of the United Methodist Church, 178-179.

- Reviews the local church's membership
- Fills in the vacancies of lay officers

- Approves the local church's budget based on the proposal from the Finance Committee
- Makes sure the church's financial needs are taken care of
- Recommends to the Charge Conference the salary and other benefits of the pastor(s) and employees of the local church based on recommendations from the staff (pastor)-parish committee.

b. The Mission and Ministry of the Church Council

All the functions of the Church Council can be summed into the following:

- Nurture
- Outreach
- Witness and Resourcing

Nurture

A Council is supposed to nurture the church to grow to its fullest potential. In carrying out this function, the Ministries of nurture focus on:

- Education
- Worship
- Christian Formation
- Membership Care
- Small Groups
- Stewardship.

Outreach

To aid in its Ministries of Outreach and mission, an Administrative Council focuses on the following:

- Compassion
- Justice, and advocacy
- Church and society
- Global Ministries
- Higher Education and Campus Ministry,
- Health and Social Welfare,
- Christian Unity & interreligious concerns
- Religion and Race,
- The Status and Role of Women

Witness

Witnessing is an important part of our call to Salvation. Christ called us to go into all the world and witness to souls. Based upon this call, churches have designed some ministries around the concept.

- "The Witness Ministries shall give attention to developing and strengthening evangelistic efforts of sharing of personal and congregational stories of Christian experience, faith, and service;
- communications;
- Lay Servant/Speaker Ministries, and other means that give expressions of witness for Jesus Christ."

o The leadership development and resourcing ministries – develops people for lay leadership as well as clergy leadership for the church.

c. The meeting time of the Church Council

The council meets at least four times a year (quarterly) at a venue and time decided upon by the church. The chairperson or the pastor may call special meetings. It is recommended that the council uses a consensus/discernment model of decision-making.

To reach consensus means that members at the meeting agreed on something without taking vote. When members at the meeting cannot reach consensus then vote shall be taken.

d. The membership of the Church Council

The Charge Conference determines the membership of the church council. The council consists of persons who represent the program ministries of the church. The membership shall include but not limited to the following:

- The chairperson of the church council;
- The lay leaders
- The chairperson and/or a representative of the committee of pastor(staff)-parish relations;
- The chairperson and/or a representative of the committee on finance;
- The chairperson and/or a representative of the board of trustees
- The church treasurer;

- A lay member to annual conference;
- The president and/or a representative of the United Methodist Men;
- The president and/or a representative of the United Methodist women;
- The president and / or a young adult representative;
- a representative of the United Methodist youth;
- the pastor(s)

e. The Quorum of the Church Council

Webster defines quorum as *"the number of officers and members of a body that when duly assembled is legally competent to transact business."*[71] In the UMC, whenever a meeting is duly announced the members present and voting at any duly announced meeting shall constitute a quorum.

[71] *Merriam Webster's Collegiate Dictionary, Tenth Edition*

CHAPTER 7

THE DUTIES OF THE LAY LEADER AND THE CHAIRPERSON OF THE CHURCH COUNCIL

Many persons in the United Methodist Church argue about the higher status between the lay leader and the chairperson of the Church Council. My thought is that both are called to serve the local church in their respective positions. These are two positions that members lobby for .

For some, these two positions are prestigious. The simple thing to understand is that the chairperson of the church council heads the administrative arm of the church while the lay leader is the head of all lay people. One thing to note is that the chairperson of the council is also a lay person and the lay leader is a part of the church council headed by the chairperson. So, both are servant leaders.

This is the key thing to note. It seems now necessary to treat the issues with the level importance it requires. Let us consider these positions separately:

The Church Lay Leader[72]

A local church lay leader is a member of the laity who has been chosen as a leader. He or she is elected yearly by the charge conference; and is a professing member of the local church.

Duties of the Lay Leader

- The primary representative of the laity in a local church.
- Fosters awareness of the role of laity both within the congregation and through their ministries in the home, workplace, community, and world, and finding ways within the community of faith to recognize all these ministries.
- Meets regularly with the pastor to discuss the state of the church and the needs for ministry.
- Assists in advising the church council of opportunities available and needs expressed for a more effective ministry of the church through its laity in the community.
- Informs the laity of training opportunities provided by the district conference as well as the annual conference.
- Attends training programs, workshops, retreats in order to strengthen his or her work. The lay leader is encouraged to become a certified lay servant.
- Must be visionary. He or she must be a dreamer.
- Must be a people-oriented or people-friendly person.
- Must be a team player.

[72] *The Book of Discipline*, 176-177.

The Church Council Chairperson[73]

The chairperson of the church council handles administrative matters. He or she is elected annually by the charge conference. He or she must be a professing member of the local church.

- Leads the council in fulfilling its responsibilities.

- Prepares and communicates the agenda of meetings in consultation with the pastor(s), lay leader and other appropriate persons.

- Reviews and assigns responsibility for implementation of actions taken by the council.

- Coordinates the various activities of the council.

- Provides the initiative and leadership for the council as it does the planning, establishing of objectives and goals, and evaluating.

- Participates in leadership training programs as offered by the annual conference and /or district.

- Attends all boards and committees meetings.

- Is encouraged to attend annual conferences.
- Coordinates with the pastor(s) and lay leaders.

[73] Ibid, 177-178.

DISCUSSION FOR REFLECTION

1. **Name at least five (5) functions of the chairperson of the church council.**

2. **Name at least five (5) functions of the church lay leader.**

CHAPTER 8

ADMINISTRATIVE & SUPPORT COMMITTEES AND MINISTRIES

There are four administrative committees. Other committees are considered as support committees. The four administrative committees are: Committee on Nominations and Leadership Development, Staff-Parish Relations Committee, Finance Committee and Board of Trustees.

Committee On Nominations And Leadership Development

The charge conference elects annually members of the committee on nominations and leadership development from professing members of the local church. This committee is to identify, develop, deploy, evaluate, and monitor Christian spiritual leadership for the local church. The committee carries out the following:

- It serves throughout the year to help the church council on issues regarding the leadership of the congregation so as to focus on mission and ministry as the context for service.

- It guides in the development and training of spiritual leaders; recruits, nurtures, and supports spiritual leaders; and assist the church council in assessing the changing leadership needs.

- It recommends to the charge conference, at its last seating, the names of people to serve as officers and leaders of the local church.

- The Membership of this committee is "not more than nine persons, in addition to the pastor and the lay leaders".

- The young adults and the youth fellowships must be represented on this committee. The senior pastor or the pastor-in-charge serves as the chairperson. A layperson has to be elected by the committee to serve as the vice chairperson.

- The membership is divided into three classes. Members in class one will serve for one year; class two for two years and class three for three years. Retiring members of the committee shall not succeed themselves. When vacancies occur during the year, nominees shall be elected by the church council with the permission of the district superintendent.

- This committee must be inclusive and diverse in its selection process.

Staff-Parish Relations Committee[74]

Members of this committee are elected yearly at the last charge conference. Professing members from the local church are elected to this committee. Members must be engaged in and attentive to their Christian spiritual development to give proper leadership in the responsibilities with which the committee is entrusted.

The composition of the Committee

This committee is made up of "not fewer than five nor more than nine persons representative of the total charge". The young adults and youth fellowships are represented on this committee. No relatives of a pastor or an employee may serve on the committee.

The Meeting of the Committee

Officially, this committee meets four times in a year. Additional meetings take place at the request of the bishop, the district superintendent, the pastor, any other person accountable to the committee, or the chairperson of the committee. No

[74] Ibid, 192-194.

meeting takes place without the consent of the pastor and /or the district superintendent. The pastor shall be present at each meeting of the committee on pastor -parish relations or staff-parish relations except where he or she voluntarily excuses himself or herself.

The committee may meet with the district superintendent without the pastor or appointed staff under consideration being present. However, the pastor or appointed staff under consideration shall be notified prior to such meeting with the district superintendent and be brought into consultation immediately thereafter. The committee shall meet in closed session, and information shared in the committee shall be confidential.

The Functions of the Committee

The duties of the committee shall include the following:

• Encourages, strengthens, nurtures, supports, and respects the pastor(s) and staff and their families.

• Promotes unity in the church(es).

• Confers with and counsels the pastor(s) and staff on the matters pertaining to the effectiveness of ministry;

• relationships with the congregation; the pastor's health and self-care, conditions that may impede the effectiveness of ministry; and to interpret the nature and function of the ministry.

• Confers with, consults, and counsels the pastor(s) and staff

▪ on matters pertaining to priorities in the use of gifts, skills,

▪ and time and priorities for the demands and effectiveness of the mission and ministry of the congregation.

• Provides evaluation at least annually for the use of the

▪ pastor(s) and staff in an ongoing effective ministry and for

▪ identifying continuing educational needs and plans.

• Communicates and interprets to the congregation the nature and function of ministry in the United Methodist Church regarding open itinerancy, the preparation for ordained ministry, and the Ministerial Education Fund.

• Develops and approves written job descriptions and titles for associate pastors and other staff members in cooperation with the senior pastor. The term associate pastor is used as a general term to indicate any pastoral appointment in a local church other than the pastor in charge. Committee shall be encouraged to develop specific titles for associate pastors that reflect the job descriptions and expectations.

• Consults with the pastor and staff concerning continuing

▪ education, work-life balance, dimensions of personal health and wellness, and spiritual renewal, arranges with the church council for the necessary time and financial assistance for the attendance of the pastor and /or staff at such continuing education, self-care, and spiritual renewal events as may serve their professional and spiritual growth, and encourages staff members to seek professional certification in their fields of specialization.

• Enlists, interviews, evaluates, reviews, and recommends

▪ annually to the charge conference lay preachers and persons for candidacy for ordained ministry.

• Interprets preparation for ordained ministry and the

▪ Ministerial Education Fund to the congregation.

• Confers with the pastor and /or other appointed members of the staff if it should become evident that the best interests of the charge and pastor(s) will be served by a change of pastor(s). It shall cooperate with the pastor(s), the district superintendent, and the bishop in securing clergy leadership. Its relationship to the district superintendent and the bishop shall be advisory only.

• Recommends to the church council, after consultation with the pastor, the professional and other staff positions

▪ (whether employee or contract) needed to carry out the work of the church or charge.

• Educates the church community on the value of diversity of selection in clergy and lay staff and develop a commitment to same.

• Members keep themselves informed of personnel matters in relationship to the Church's policy, professional standards, liability issues, and civil law. They are responsible for communicating and interpreting such matters to staff.

▪ Committee members should make themselves available for educational and training opportunities provided by the conference, district, and /or other arenas that will enable them to be effective in their work.

▪ Consults on matters pertaining to pulpit supply, proposals for compensation, travel expense, vacation, health and life insurance, pension, housing (which may be a church-owned parsonage or housing allowance in lieu of parsonage if in compliance with the policy of the annual conference), and other practical matters effecting the work and families of the pastor and staff, and make annual recommendations regarding such matters to the church council, reporting budget items to the committee on finance.

▪ Encourages, monitors, and supports clergy and lay staff pursuit health and wholeness.

The Finance Committee[75]

The charge conference elects a Finance Committee annually from the recommendation of the committee on nominations and leadership development or from the floor. Membership of the committee constitutes the following:

[75] Ibid, 197-199.

- the chairperson;
- the pastor(s);
- a lay member of the annual conference;
- the chairperson of the church council;
- the chairperson or representative of the committee on pastor(staff)-parish relations;
- a representative of the trustees to be selected by the trustees,
- the chairperson of the ministry group on stewardship;
- the lay leader;
- the financial secretary;
- the treasurer;
- the church business administrator(if there is any);
- and other members to be added as the charge conference may determine.

One person should not hold the position of treasurer and financial secretary. Members serving as treasurer and financial secretary should not be immediate family members.

Functions of the Committee:

▪ Gives stewardship of financial resources as their priority throughout the year.

• Strategizes, and implements ways to generate more resources for mission and ministries of local churches and beyond.

▪ Finds creative ways to turn their congregation into tithing congregations with an attitude of generosity.

• Prepares and submits annual budget to the Church council for approval.

• Designates at least two persons not of the immediate family residing in the same household to count the offering.

▪ Makes sure funds received be deposited promptly in accordance with the procedures established by the committee on finance. The financial secretary shall keep records of the contributions and payments.

▪ The church treasurer(s) shall disburse all funds contributed to causes represented in the local church budget, and such other funds and contributions as the church council may determine.

• Establishes written financial policies to document the internal controls of the local church. The written financial policies should be reviewed for adequacy and effectiveness annually by the committee on finance and submitted as a report to the charge conference annually.

▪ Makes provision for an annual audit of the financial statements of the local church and all its organizations and accounts. A local church audit is defined as an independent evaluation of the financial reports and records and the internal controls of the local church by a qualified person or persons.

▪ The audit shall be conducted for the purpose of reasonably verifying the reliability of financial reporting, determine whether assets are being safeguarded, and determining compliance with local law, local church policies and procedures, and the Book of Discipline.

• The committee shall recommend to the church council proper depositories for the church's funds. Funds received shall be deposited promptly in the name of the local church.

• Contributions designated for specific causes and objects shall be promptly forwarded according to the intent of the donor and shall not be used for any other purpose.

▪ After the budget of the local church has been approved, additional appropriations or changes in the budget must be approved by the council.

• The committee shall prepare annually a report to the church council of all designated funds that are separate from the current expense budget.

Board of Trustees

Members of the board of trustees are elected annually by the charge conference. Membership of the board may consist of a chairperson, vice chairperson, secretary and a treasurer.

Meeting of Local Church Board of Trustees

Meeting takes place at the call of the pastor or of its chairperson at least annually at such times and place as shall be designated in a notice to each trustee and the pastor(s) at a reasonable time prior to the appointed time of meeting. A majority of the members of the board of trustees shall constitute a quorum.

Functions of the Board of Trustees

• Supervision, oversight, and care of all real property owned by the local church and of all property and equipment acquired directly by the local church.

• Reviews annually the adequacy of the property, liability, and crime insurance coverage on church owned property,

▪ buildings, and equipment.

▪ When a pastor and /or a board of trustees are asked to grant permission to an outside organization to use church facilities, permission can be granted only when such use is consistent with the Social principles and ecumenical objectives.

▪ Reviews the church-owned parsonage to ensure proper maintenance.

▪ Receives and administers all trust; and shall invest all trust funds of the local church in conformity with the laws of the country, state, or like political unit in which the local church is located.

• Acts as a socially responsible investor and reports annually to the charge conference regarding its carrying out of this responsibility.

Support Committees

Support committees are simply committees in addition to the administrative committees. They help in carrying out other ministry activities in the local congregation. The committees may include:

Committee on Communications

- Is headed by a chairperson and a co-chairperson.
- Coordinates the radio and television ministries and other media activities of the local congregation.

- Works with both print and electronic media as it relates to interviews with the leadership of the church, advertisements, and radio talk shows, among others.

Committee on Records and History

- A chairperson and a co-chairperson head this committee.
- writes and updates the history of the local congregation.
- preserves the history of the local church.
- clothed with the authority to teach members about the church – from whence the church has come, its spiritual as well its temporal growth among others.

Committee on Health

- is headed by a chairperson and a co-chairperson.
- Provides first aid for members in emergency cases
- Provides healthcare education to members of the church

Committee on Worship

- is headed by a chairperson and a co-chairperson
- plans worship activities and ensures the worship is Wesleyan.
- explains to the congregation the different Christian seasons and their significances.
- Makes sure that every worship service is relevant and is meeting the spiritual need of the congregation.

Committee on Education and Scholarship

• Is headed by a chairperson and a co-chairperson

• focuses on educational matters.

• handles all educational and scholarship matters of the church.

• sets guidelines concerning who needs financial aids and scholarship.

• evaluates everyone who applies for financial aids as well as scholarship.

• monitors students' progress and report same to the church council.

• makes sure that everyone on financial aid or scholarship brings in his or her academic report regularly.

• clothed with the authority to counsel with the students.

Committee on Evangelism and Missions

• evangelism, revivals, crusades and church planting are major things that are done by this committee.

• clothed with the authority to organize evangelistic campaigns that will draw people to Jesus the Christ.

• It can also write, print and distribute evangelistic tracts.

Family Life Ministry

• Is headed by a chairperson and a co-chairperson

• Should be headed by someone who is married and has a good family life.

• plans and implements training sessions for married couples

• assists the pastors to do post-marital counseling as well as pre-marital counseling

- intervenes and prays with married couples in difficult times.
- Coordinates all activities in relation to couples
- Conducts special prayer sessions for couples and others

Committee on Social Concerns

- is headed by a chairperson and a co-chairperson
- meets the social needs of members
- pays regular visits to aged, troubled, and the bereaved.

Committee on Music

- handles all activities of music; supervises the various choirs.
- ensures that directors are ably teaching and leading the choirs
- ensures that music are appropriate and relevant.
- ensures that discipline is the hallmark of the ministry
- recruits members for the choirs
- ensures that relevant musical instruments are available
- organizes workshop and seminars for the choirs

Advance Committee

- A chairperson and a co-chairperson lead this committee
- plans and implements fundraising activities for the local church.
- Financial strategist of the local congregation

Membership Committee

- A chairperson and a co-chairperson supervises this committee
- keeps records of the church's membership

- carries out update of the membership roll
- engages in visitation
- establishes phone directory – phone numbers and addresses of members

Harvest Committee

- The committee is headed by a chairperson and co-chairperson
- Plans for the church's thanksgiving harvest
- Encourages people to bring their first fruits in thanksgiving to God
- Coordinates and represents the church at district harvest program

Ushering Ministry

- This ministry is headed by a president and other officers who are elected by the ushers and usherettes.
- Serves as the protocol officers for and during the worship service.

The Legal Advisory Committee

- This committee is composed of church members with legal background. It is headed by a chairperson and a co-chairperson.
- Provides legal counsel to the church on legal matters
- Provides legal education to church members especially in regards to the United Methodist Social Principles.

- Represents the church when the church is faced with some legal problems .

Connectional Ministries

- Responsible to focus and guide the mission and ministry of the local church
- Serve as steward of the vision of the church including development , clarification, interpretation, and embodiment of the vision
- Serve as leader of the continuous process of transformation and renewal necessary for the local church to be faithful to our Christian identity in a changing world

- Ensure the connections among the organizations and ministry agencies for the purpose of networking, resourcing and communicating their shared ministry

- Provide encouragement, coordination and support for ministries of nurture, outreach and witness in the local church

- Ensure the alignment of total resources of the local church to its mission.

- Plans and evaluates the ministries of the local church

- Ensure that that planning retreat takes place every year.

NB. These are few of the support committees. Each local church may add as per its ministry activities.

Specialized Ministries[76]

In the UMC, there are several ministries that are carried on. Some include: ***Ministry to the aged, Children Ministry, Family Life Ministry, ushering ministry, acolyte ministry,*** *Ministry* ***to the physically challenged, young people ministries, Singles Ministry, Campus ministry, etc.***

The Church School [77]

The church school is the teaching arm of the local church. It is established for accomplishing the church's educational ministry. It is challenged to create communities in which people of all ages experience God's active presence in their lives; foster health, nonviolent relationships within the congregation and community; testify to the reconciling love of God through Christ; and live out their faith in the world as witness to the coming of the reign of God. It is headed by a superintendent who is elected by the charge conference.

[76] Ibid, 180.
[77] Ibid, 182.

DISCUSSION FOR REFLECTION

1. Name the four administrative committees

2. Give five functions of the SPRC.

3. Give three functions of the finance committee

4. Who chairs the committee on nominations and leadership development.

5. Name at least five support committees.

CHAPTER 9

KEY ORGANIZATIONS IN A LOCAL UNITED METHODIST CHURCH

There are five key organizations in the local church: the United Methodist Men, the United Methodist Women, the United Methodist Young Adults Fellowship and the United Methodist Youth Fellowship and the children. Everyone in a local church belongs to one of these groups.

UNITED METHODIST MEN[78]

United Methodist Men is the official organization for men (male from 31 years and above) in the United Methodist Church

[78] Ibid, 189-190.

at the local church, district, and annual conference levels. This organization shall be organized in every local United Methodist Church.

Purpose of the United Methodist Men:

The United Methodist Men's organization exists to declare the centrality of Christ in every man's life.

- To involve men in a growing relationship to Jesus the Christ and his church.
- To provide resources and support for programs of evangelism focused on the needs of men.
- To promote resources and programs in the area of Stewardship.
- To develop men to take up leadership responsibility in a local church.

Additionally, the United Methodist Men should engage in Christian service. Membership to this body is open to any who desires to belong and participate in the ministry of the church through the United Methodist men. The pastors are ex-officio members of the unit and its executive committee.

This group is to raise funds to carry out its purpose; and all funds from whatever source secured by the united Methodist men's unit belong to the organization and shall be disbursed only in accordance with its constitution and / or by-laws and by its order. It may have its own bank accounts; and shall have an annual financial audit.

The unit has the authority to elect its own officers. The officers to be elected include but not limited to the following: president, vice-president, secretary, financial secretary, treasurer, chaplain, etc.

UNITED METHODIST WOMEN[79]

United Methodist women organization is the official organization for women (females from 31 years and above) in the United Methodist Church at the local church, district, and annual conference levels. This organization shall be organized in every local United Methodist Church.

Purpose

- A community of women whose purpose is to know God and to experience freedom as whole persons through Jesus Christ; to develop a creative, supportive fellowship; and to expand concepts of mission through participation in the global ministries of the church.

Membership

Membership is open to any woman who indicates her desire to belong and to participate in the global mission of the church through United Methodist Women. The pastor(s) shall be ex officio member of the local unit and of its executive committee.

Leadership

The unit shall elect a president, a vice president, a secretary, a treasurer, and a committee on nominations. Additional officers and committees shall be elected or appointed as needed, in accordance with the plans of the United Methodist Women's national organization as set forth in the bylaws for the local unit of United Methodist Women.

---

[79] Ibid, 187-188.

Funding

• United Methodist Women shall secure funds for the fulfillment of its purpose.

• All funds from whatever source secured by the unit of the United Methodist Women belong to the organization and shall be disbursed only in accordance with its constitution and by its order.

• The women shall make an annual pledge to the total budget of the district or conference organization of United Methodist Women.

Meeting

This group meets at the time designated for implementing its purpose and transacting its business as the unit itself shall decide.

Relationship to the Local Church

The unit is to encourage all women to participate in the total life and work of the Church and to support them in assuming positions of responsibility and leadership.

UNITED METHODIST YOUNG PEOPLE'S MINISTRIES [80]

The young people's ministries in the United Methodist Church consist of youths and young adults. Young adults' age range is from 19 years thru 30 years while youths' age range is from 12 years thru 18 years. Both fellowships are given the authority to elect their own leadership under the guidance of

---

[80] Ibid, 184-185.

their respective coordinators. Those to be elected are but not limited to the following: president, vice president, secretary, financial secretary, treasurer, etc.

The fellowships operate at the local church, district and annual conference levels. The council governs these groups on Youths and Young adults ministries. Members serve on the leadership team in local churches, district and annual conferences.

CHILDREN'S MINISTRIES[81]

The children's ministry is made up of children up to eleven years of age. Ministries for, with, and by children include all ministries involving children within the life of the congregational community, including but not limited to Sunday school, vacation Bible school, nursery ministries, children's choir and music ministries, fellowship groups, support groups, short-term study groups, children's worship experience, mission education experiences, intergenerational activities, and all weekday programs for children of all ages. It is headed by a coordinator.

[81] Ibid, 183.

DISCUSSION FOR REFLECTION

1. NAME THE FIVE MAJOR GROUPINGS IN A LOCAL UNITED METHODIST CHURCH.

2. DISCUSS TWO THINGS ABOUT THE UNITED METHODIST WOMEN ORGANIZATION.

3. DISCUSS AT LEAST THREE SPECIALIZED MINISTRIES

SAVIOR, LIKE A SHEPHERD LEAD US

Savior, like a shepherd lead us,
Much we need thy tender care;
In thy pleasant pastures feed us,
For our use thy folds prepare;
Blessed Jesus, blessed Jesus!
Thou has bought us, thine we are.

We are thine, do thou befriend us,
Be the guardian of our way;
Keep thy flock, from sin defend us,
Seek us when we go astray;
Blessed Jesus blessed Jesus!
Hear, O hear us, when we pray.

Thou has promised to receive us,
Poor and sinful though we be;
Thou has mercy to relieve us,
Grace to cleanse and power to free;
Blessed Jesus blessed Jesus!
We will early turn to thee.

Early let us seek thy favor,
Early let us do thy will;
Blessed Lord and only Savior,
With thy love our bosoms fill;
Blessed Jesus blessed Jesus!
Thou has loved us, love us still.   Amen

The hymn was written by Dorothy A. Thrupp and music by William B. Bradbury.

EVERY LEADER NEEDS TO PRAY THIS SONG:

I AM THINE, O LORD

1. I am thine, O Lord, I have heard thy voice
And it told thy love to me,
But I long to rise in the arms of faith,
And be closer drawn to Thee.

Refrain: Draw me nearer, nearer, blessed Lord
To thy cross where thou has died;
Draw me nearer, nearer, blessed Lord
To thy precious bleeding side.

2. Consecrate me now to thy service, Lord,
By the power of grace divine;
Let my soul look up with a steadfast hope,
And my will be lost in thine.

3. O the pure delight of a single hour.
That before thy throne I spend,
When I kneel in prayer, and with thee, my God,
I commune as friend with friend!

The hymn was written by Fanny J. Crosby and music by William H. Doane.

Author's Note

Thanks for reading this little book. I hope it has helped you understand leadership from biblical context. I also pray that you were blessed to get insights about the local church and how it goes about carrying out its different functions and ministries.

This book is meant to broaden your understanding about the pastorate and its functions; the church council and its functions as well as the duties of the church lay leader and the church council chairperson.

Administrative and support committees have been looked at to help you know workable committees in the local congregation.

In the UMC, we have five major groups. These groups have been discussed to give you a better understanding of how they work and how they are related to the local church

BIBLIOGRAPHY

Ammerman, Nancy T. *Studying Congregations: A New Handbook.* Nashville: Abingdon Press, 1998.

Anderson, Robert C. *Effective Pastor: A Practical Guide to Ministry.* Chicago: Moody Press, 1998.

Baab , Lynne M. *Embracing Midlife Congregations as Support Systems.* Virginia: Alban Institute Publication, 1999.

Blackaby, Henry & Richard. *Spiritual Leadership.* Nashville: B & H Publishing Group, 2001

Barna, George . *Leaders on Leadership.* California: Regal Books, 1997.

Callahan, Kennon, L. *Small, Strong Congregations-Creating Strengths and Health for Your Congregation.* San Francisco, Jossey-Bass, 2000.

Cox. Sr. J. Larmark. *A Handbook for Conference, District and Local Church Leaders.* Georgia: SCP /Third World Literature Publishing House, 1994.

Dennison, Justin. *Team Ministry:A Blueprint for Christian Leadership.* Great Britain: OM Books, 1997.

Dudley, Carl S. et al. *Carriers of Faith: Lessons from Congregational Studies.* Louisville: Westminster/John Konox Press, 1991.

Fitts, Sr., Bob. *Acts-The House Church: The New Testament Model for Multiplying Congregations.* Volume 30, no.2 (April/May/June 2002): 1-7

Floding, Matthew. *Welcome To Theological Field Education.* Virginia: The Alban Institute, 2011.

Harmon, Nolan B. *Understanding The United Methodist Church.* Nashville: Parthenon Press, 1983.

Heward-Mills, Dag. *Church Planting.* Wellington: Lux Verbi.BM (Pty) Ltd., 2008.

Heward-Mills, Dag. *The Successful Leader.* Accra: Parchment House, 2002.

Heward-Mills, Dag. *The Art of Leadership.* Accra: Parchment House, 2003.

Hillman, Jr., George M. *Ministry Greenhouse: Cultivating Environments for Practical Learning.* Virginia: The Alban Institute, 2008.

Hopewell, James F. *Congregation: Stories and Structures.* Philadelphia: Fortress Press, 1987.

Kouzes, James M. and Barry Z. Posner. *The Leadership Challenge.* San Francisco: Jossey-Bass Publishers, 1995.

Malphurs, Aubrey. *Look Before You Lead: How To Discern and Shape Your Church Culture.* Grand Rapids: Baker Books, 2013.

Maxwell, John C. *Developing the Leader Within You.* Nashville: Thomas Nelson, Inc., 1993.

O'Donovan, Wilber. *Biblical Christianity in An African Perspective.* Ilorin: The Nigeria Evangelical Fellowship, 1992

Nelson, C. Ellis. *Congregations: Their Power To Form and Transform.* Atlanta: John Knox Press, 1988.

Sanders, J. Oswald. *Spiritual Leadership: Commitment to Spiritual Growth Series.* London: Authentic Books, 1994.

Slater, Robert. *29 Leadership Secrets from Jack Welch*. New York: McGraw-Hill, 2003

The Book of Discipline of The United Methodist Church, Nashville: The United Methodist Publishing House , 2012.

Thompson, George B. *How To Get Along with Your Church: Creating Cultural Capital for Doing Ministry*. Cleveland: The Pilgrim Press, 2001.

Thompson, George B. *Treasures in Clay Jars: New Ways To Understand Your Church.* Eugene: Wipf and Stock Publishers, 2003.

Warford,.Malcolm. *Becoming A New Church-Reflections on Faith and Calling*. Ohio: United Church Press, 2000.

Weems, Jr., Lovett W. *Take The Next Step – Leading Lasting Change in the Church.* Nashville: Abingdon Press, 2003.

Weems, Jr., Lovett W. & Anna A. Michel. The Crisis of Young Clergy.Nashville: Abingdon Press, 2008.

ABOUT THE AUTHOR

Dr. Julius Y.Z. K. Williams, I is a clergy person of the Liberia Annual Conference of the United Methodist Church. He is currently serving as the Pastor of the First United Methodist Church of the Monrovia District Conference.

He is married to Tonya Gbelia Williams; and the union is blessed with three children: Julius Jay, Julton Praise and Julianne Mona.

Dr. Williams holds an Associate Degree in Accounting from the A.M.E. Zion Community College, a B.Th. in General Theology from the United Methodist University; a M.Th. in Pastoral Theology from the Cuttington Graduate School and a Doctor of Ministry from the Wesley Theological Seminary. He also holds an advanced certificate in leadership.

He has served as Program and Financial Officer of the Department of Evangelism and Missions, LAC/UMC; Associate and Senior Pastor of the New Georgia UMC; Pastor of the Grace United Methodist Church. He is a facilitator at the Liberia International Leadership Institute.

He is the co-author of Triumphs of Grace- A Membership Manual for the Liberia Annual Conference. He is the author of The Life of a Mom and Ministry Partner.

OTHER TITLES BY THE AUTHOR

Triumphs of Grace- A Membership Manual for the Liberia Annual Conference.

The Life of a Mom and Ministry Partner

www.ingramcontent.com/pod-product-compliance
Lightning Source LLC
Chambersburg PA
CBHW071143090426
42736CB00012B/2210
* 9 7 8 0 9 9 4 6 3 0 8 3 4 *